I0110868

cuplet.

The Clambake

Cuplet 2018 Anthology

Edited by
Claire Albrecht

PUNCHER & WATTMANN

First published in 2018

Published by Puncher and Wattmann
PO Box 279
Waratah NSW 2298

http://www.puncherandwattmann.com
puncherandwattmann@bigpond.com

A catalogue record for this
book is available from the
NATIONAL
LIBRARY
OF AUSTRALIA
National Library of Australia

ISBN 9781925780390

Cover design by Claire Albrecht

*For everyone who has taken
a drink from the cup.*

Contents

CHRIS BROWN

■

village pieces (iii)

the leafy borough's

        leafage at the grate
        static on the waves

   hard sell   neuro

                plastic
     ity

        via the capital

     head up –

for the lack

   a way in

   we'll take

   it! if

     a touring welsh chorus
     humours the praetorian

      guard among us –

        personifying

take it!

just now

the breadline
out the door

at Uprising

quiet   but answers at

our feet   where sparrows dare

or walking
and some lyceen or local saint posts

a rainbow heart   at the
red letterbox

daily
we await its erasure…dissent and no
one to de

face it?

yea or nay

but auguring a
c

CHRISTOPHER BROWN

■

b (collect

ive

best)

this café

replays of yesterday

out of the shadows

loyals
locals

take a chance

whisk their
crumbs and alms

to roost

Maps of my transitory past

(May in Melbourne)

I hand the blue pleated curtain to the fleeting
Feeling a bit abused the way the cabin looked
After fifteen hours but leaving nothing behind.
Open spaces then the grid and tilt to shelves of
Vacant strata (loading...) some exposed scopic
Ledge at a misty lean. This precinct has sharp
Teeth but not for pedestrians less *Les Pietons
De Mai!* Fresh even now. Skaters' idle grace
In the park of countermeasures and collared
Elms and stairs stacking up to soft concrete
Landings. Only so much order. Not a regular
Knave among the artists merchants purvey
Ors. But ask any blind cop: in a matraquage
There's nought to see and we'd better run. A
Long. Days of rain. The gutters refuse the
stars and stare out to sea. We offer feed
back we mend the greener strips of the
Broken cycleway breach twin rail to the
Gendered dorm of a converted nunnery.
It isn't half the exile it used to be. Cosmo
Polites keep the oddest hours communal
Bookcases the best of hugo for a rainy day.
Cities patch our coats cry *proust* for cheers.
It pays to update the folks to pin these and
Other relics to your graphic trail the weight
Less map of your immediate transitory past.

MICHELLE CAHILL

Ruins

St Andrews

'little shuffling sound as of a nearly dried-up woman'
                              ~ Alice Oswald

whose silences hammered   the skies' apse
                        gaps in heaven
whose hand scriptures   prescient to my
               weeping   wincing,
I am sodden, I am sunk   in cold grass, the quire
      unsung,   careening, I lull   a broken tenor—

fulmars score the nave   for wind worms ,
light streaming   a dress, stockings   a summer scarf

wind puckering gravestones   picks clean the relics

        how   pitiable to sleep   to drown
my creaking breath   little gasping sound,
        little sweet thirst   velvet liturgy—
error of lips,   little shivering   my shivering

I knew   (... say what you like)   I never

Forbidden City?

Morning is shuttered, and we are like dormant fireflies
at the river's edge, pale sky, the dainty fruit of miniature
orange blossom—say I'm not banished, then block me.
Texting isn't my dialect tho I want your revolving heart.
And how little I would want to lose the scent of your hair
brushing fingertips with a Princess from the provinces.
Confess I have been using Express VPN; it's pretty good.
You said Shakira's 'Don't Bother' wasn't your type.
You definitely have a love-hate relationship with my body.
The river is a dark filigree in moonlight; the library at
the Pavilion of Literary Profundity has black, watery tiles.
All the other roofs are yellow, but how green is the Prince?
Night vendors of silk-worm cocoons and sea horse kebabs
take cash or WeChat credit, opium poppies blousy the lake.
Jian bing for brekky; soy 'n egg-smeared coriander flakes.
They crackle, gag, feet bound, legs tied back, the sous-chef
in the galley is masked, serving mussels, steamed oysters.
After thin-wheeled bicycles, pink southern lychees, a court
seals the probate, painted fan, calligraphy of sweet lies.

A.J. CARRUTHERS

■

Two pages from EvFL Stanzas

Page 1

| Eíla drank Potensac,
- imperial rouge in Tophet, rigidrosedisks: goorde
- gripped
- array! originality aufgestöhrt-assailing
- sedgerocked fromupon hornèd wore earsplitting
        shininginexuberance
- in electrapturous mechanical, rotate blank
- new rudern rudern everywheretruant zu zur
- great greatpossession flare
-
-

| Eyes seestsawest crimson crimsón hidden hiddén hidden
- immobile of stonymystery like mine glare
- ——

- just sipping, contra immodesttoilets
- estate sharp changeling!outspread mixed from barbér things
- indecentclerk incarnate
- ——

- jewels
- aristocracy unhampered, tri-ri-ri molecules tri-ri-ri surrender
-

| Enigma oozes
- boisterous tremendous concentrate pleases dánce, pleases
        surprísing education, alarm
- bubble windbags-storage-grace dockhand
- sick printersink companionship! sousedvoluptuous birchness
- placedomeages! "information-nichtmared"

- astatootch-assembled grief, distortion information
- ty —
-
-
-

| Europe is Bloodmoney, inexpressive luckily in interested occasion
- xidneppA
- constitution's mechanical Cloudhole
- earigidthflight edge
- nostrils Cortège stubblefield
- tépid rosetinsel glint wasterestlintakeg Points Traditional
- rim giltinsel
- insect
- curlyfrail is zirp pal!
-

Page 2

| lollt Elsius, lollt Pilatus
- lonely   accomplishing, grimsweat thinemesh
- logic accomplishes
- upbear, would flimflam without
- panicky-checkless, róisterer
-
-
-
-
-

A.J. CARRUTHERS

■

| light — Manikin:
- a-va-jDuna romes — — dippedlightipped Out
- redtopped Jonathan turned Jonathan Spýgauzy, brilliant in
        Strokelings
- kroo! radiocaparisoned eyepoint, mulish Into Tore — —
        Chalkwhite — — — —
- léaped addréss, emptyindifferent
- is repetition Tidelaw thence—
- flurry
- einKlang!
-
-

| luxury livest, motionless and Zweifellosigkeit!, uptilted-glassy!
- im. ind. hversemisphere* All bluntindustry All
        perceptiondispelling penury monotony (*OY)
- moony ás time
- pondering Yon SOdbrend, upcrest Galore Flagged Clime, faintly
- incarnate malignant along Tormalinde, slate-green
- dimpled set emeroyd. stark-tápery, sharp:
- emeroyd singeing — Alaugh — stark —
- yesterday's routine? wintry-upon-appendicitis, architecture
- ee — ee Automatonguts — ee — ee Systematical — ee —
- demon's digestive Scirremorselesshous Instinctive Stifflepant!
| likeness exists since Precision, monotonous annihilating A-bláb
        — A-shátter — áttar —
- atop —
- kissclangor, Toll—
- erethought 'Och!'
- logic's halodrummerflavor Soft-of-mistake

- exhilirating Communion-Milkshake served tastes, únmasking
      'Genickstarre — '
- von
- emerald Tinweep Arist
- lymphatic Saint presses avec Kyk! Marcelled From pneumatic Light —
- semi-SapPansyhireSoftilence, spatted-Leafy, Netted pínk In Natty
      Travesty-Looms —

Memento Vivere Baroness Elsa von Freytag-Loringhoven

AMELIA DALE

■

blood results 6/24

Blood on paper 170 x 170 mm

blood results 15/24

Blood on paper 170 x 170 mm

TRICIA DEARBORN

The changes

Kissing Louise was a bell. Unlike
the chimes of the genteel drawing-room clock
it gave no warning before it struck.

It was more like the shock of the extra-early
morning alarm
on the day of the journey.

Or the sudden shrilling of a schoolroom bell,
calling me in
to a strange new lesson.

It rang sweet as a tardy dinner gong
summoning me to a meal
of scent and heat.

Resonated like a great church bell
calling the villagers over fields
to christenings, to benedictions.

My throat sang my body
swung my skin shone
and my old life shivered and fell from me

and lay like the sweat of the ringers in the tower.

[74] Tungsten

From the sequence 'Autobiochemistry'

sudden dusk
in the house again
my hand at the light switch

it's always one of those
old black bakelite switches
that click so distinctly

click! the filament
fails to blaze, an ominous
absence of incandescence

I run from switch to switch
each click! floods a room
with nightmare dark

TRICIA DEARBORN

■

Therapist, dreamt

The night after the second session
we walk through spacious dream-rooms,
talking. In future instalments

you talk about Jung on the sofa at the party.
We stand at a fence, looking in at
some wild greenery.

You call me darling. Cook me pikelets.
You're pregnant.
You speak beautiful French.

I'm running late for a session and the toilet
is full of socks.
Your hair is dark when you are blonde,

you're black when you are white.
You wear a terrible cloth cap that doesn't suit you,
a hat that makes you look like Miss Marple.

You have two bloodless gashes on your face.
My glass of water
spills into your fireplace.

In the kitchen of my childhood home
I make you tea.
You're in our bathroom

where the mirror should be.
You're a terrier. You lean to nibble
the belly of the small furred creature

that wriggles luxuriously at your side.
You're in the dream with the very small plum tree
surprisingly in blossom.

We are almost always in the same country,
the same room. Once
in the same bed

where you held me safely as I slept
so my body could remember. Another time,
we strip. You're going to help me

warm the frozen person
who gripped my hand and was hauled up
from under the sand under the ocean.

BENJAMIN DODDS

Claire

With both hands I prise apart
my sister's jaws She's mad
with biting and by now I've
had enough We share
the bed for economy
a way to live it up aboard
and abroad For the most part
she's perfectly behaved
wouldn't hassle a gnat but
possession acts up in port
When she's like this I don't
sleep lest she open my throat
Fitfully we drift in and out
a night tied alongside
a night of teeth
and bile I'm
her brother and I
love her so

[Published in *Australian Poetry Anthology* Volume 6, 2018]

Eve Incurs God's Displeasure

After Marc Chagall

There she lies
red and engorged
taking up the scene's bottom-third
like a throbbing tiger prawn.
God above is green and great and accusatory
stabbing a fat cartoon finger
at her shielded breast.
She's taken the hue of overhanging fruit
as a rudimentary deer
or something equally innocent
looks on.

Marc Chagall, Eve Incurs God's Displeasure
(from Drawings for the Bible, Verve Vol. X, M.236)
1960, colour lithograph, 35cm x 25cm.

[Published in *Cordite*, No Theme VII]

■

Disturbance

The lawless
whooping
involuntary riot
born of this lost
and panicked bird
that's brought
its wretched chaos
into the classroom's
labelled
straightened void
is one
my whole body
recognises
remembers
yet I persist
with the
futility of
quietening
them
down.

[Published in *Tincture*, Issue 7]

Evening of the Bot Man

(a bad lip reading of Rimbaud)

it's possible I'll never come down from this
high like a halo
                               lips no longer sentient
pixelations popping

am a cortisone portal u can click thru

            newly equipped for the post-whatever
my local
vocal chords pour blue from cathode displays

                  that angle back my hell to me
& yours to u

                         so encrypt me
w/ a melee of the flowers in panthers' eyes

glaciers
those bruised necrophiliacs
                     hide echoes
             & fondle the golfing brain

a single sexy night saw me regret
                  the fallout of my life
's pleasure dome
               u shivered non-plussed
the Furies all slow-clapped
our marriage
                 tweeting pics

TOBY FITCH

■

                    of the cooked-black rain
                                    the phone was
what the poem had to become
a disaster
                              i blamed our glitchy star
infused w/ lactose
                    for virtually devouring the ozone
w/ a swipe   my giant
serpents devolved
                        their vents became ineffable
ailed in an instant
                    like parfait / martyrs / time zones

like icy poles exalting
                        among purple columns of lard
& cars being edged

            & curving for kilometres thru the air

my juvy soul-view bestows a mystical horror
on these events
                        which illuminate the LOL
                                    fragments of
tiny violins still pealing from
my puerile act
                        my base monetary eyes
my blue seas of advertising

fountains guffawed from my cataracts
                no longer delirious i vommed up
                            so much big data

the government had to grapple w/ new
dispersal systems

                       my hippocampi got ex
pectorated into the night

           July fizzing w/ quadrupeds
                    crueler for their tics
my gender a genre sinking
in lieu
                  of behemoths who'd rut
maelstroms who'd pay epic amounts

           to file their regrets away into bodies
& the eternal buildings of Europe

they invaded archipelagoes of clouds
                & i provided tech support

     love needs a narrative to absorb

     the moon is atrocious w/ its solar mains
you & i both know
             desire is beastly in the flesh

& so we're content
         all the better to awkward you w/

night-night selfie
            on the bed next to me
        yr disappointment eyes

TOBY FITCH

■

Occupy the Sky

it has come to our attention that you have not
paid your death for some time as a result
of the lost world you eek out or about in
we would like to offer you the app to opt back in
to the opera shuns we funnelled you thru
you don't need to run it by or around your shelves
there are underlings available to shoulder the boredom
at a discount height they can dwarf & branch
stack your aggregate in a safe haven
just say the word & we'll pass mustard to you
pass words to you pass the castle again thru the sky pass wind
& you can occupy said Cloud again
get to know how technology works the ozone
sure l'Azur is here to stay if you don't
pay the agreed settlement amountain by the due date
this offer is w/drawn & you will have no other hopetion
but to live your own life accordingly once
cleared funds have been received you may then (or in august)
resurrect your excess gain access to our coffers
outsource your wife pay off the dog send your kids
to Upper Echelons Inc. /// can't settle?
call our orifice to concuss your hopetions
w/ one of our operatters & a void
any further contact w/ your account ants

[Published in *Ibis House* 2018]

Friday Feels

A Watt St immunologist is up on 80 sexual assault
charges as a local artist tapestries You Filthy Bastard
onto a chux, FRIGHT & FLIGHT onto his pillows.
I'm so conflicted by this session's trend in undergraduate lingo
—personally, I feel… (Bernie Sanders is too idealistic).
Increasing exposure to other people's perspectives
producing empathy as a shield.

What is a normal commodity?
At what point on the pack or lock-out?
Like a mini-mental exam to spell world backward.
Is it *schadenfreude* to want Wentconnex to deadlock
King Street, Newtown (not King St, Newcastle)?

In Monaco, there's a stunning Torres Strait Islander roof-top
mosaic—spinning our noses around to find our cringing faces.

[Published in *Newcastle Sonnets*, Glramondo 2018]

KERI GLASTONBURY

Manchester

The coda's harmonic
cadence after London Grammar, then

strolling Manchester in a thrift store
flanno, stopping for a pint in a Victorian
era underground toilet (Q as folk).

There's a beluga in a Thames
shipping lane, the individual case
a lost unit of white sensate.

The whole carriage eating crisps,
drinking gin from a tin.   I hear

there's also a Lass O'Gowrie
in this city where
post-industrial buildings
                    want to be adored.

Whitley Bay

Listening to Christine & The Queens
in a L'occitane bath,
      ingesting the cod
      from Riley's Fish Shack.

The 90 Fathom Dyke
a major crack in the earth's crust
as if it was 14 million years
of lesbian pizza ago.

           Greyhounds on Cullercoats
make me think of Tilly
(not Catherine Cookson).

The Tynemouth outdoor pool
is in ruins, like an amphitheatre or
      an anathema.

JANETTE HOPPE

■

let's give them something to talk about

this may be as good as it gets
it's an odd moment
when your surgeon tells you
you're the talk of the town

I have been that girl before

this injury has aged me
and I'm not one
who's afraid of ageing
or dying

we all need that chance to see each other
the living
the dead
and the somewhere in betweens

I am more woke
than I ever was
on the cusps
of my chronic pain opioid death
knowing is only true knowing
when death is your friend

the surgeon tells me
I will need another operation
and that it's possible
that this may be permanent

the lame leg
that doesn't know it's a leg
flounders around like a dying fish
needs a moment
to come online
the space between walking
and dying
caught at the bend
of the knee
broken

I have been that girl before

JANETTE HOPPE

a letter to my brother's wife

it must be killing you
to have a daughter
that is so much like me
head strong, outspoken,
heart on her sleeve
like the great lovers

the great ones fall hard
their love is like oxygen
and there can only ever be one
or what is the point?

your daughter
probably doesn't even know
she's like me
she doesn't even really know me
because you made sure of that

does it torment you
when she acts like me?
when she speaks out like me?
when she refuses to listen like me?
when she loves like me?
falling so hard
that she just can't breathe

suffocating
under your lack of oxygen

JANETTE HOPPE

lamb roast on Sunday

I have cut a pound of flesh
for each time he touched me
carved chicken scratches into skin
flesh of my flesh
blood of my blood

I swallowed each of his
freshly groomed words
with their serrated edges
digging
deeply into my throat
silencing the lamb I once was
before sending me to the
slaughter house of innocence

I emerged a wolf
but not in sheep's clothing
a she wolf in all of my finery
savage
with sharpened teeth
poised for his jugular
my own
meticulously groomed justice
ready to dish out
an abattoir's death

■

Five Reviews for Lars Von Trier

Breaking The Waves
Waves break through the emotional and mental challenge. A childish woman and hard wind. This too has a golden heart, much like the next one. I wouldn't watch beyond the following frame if it weren't for the handsome man who enters her bathroom. Morals batter the hull of an oil-rig until the last line arrives — which is also the first — covered in silk and hitched over her hips: the chime of dark organs nearby.

Dogville
This is a formal experiment that knows film is not a kind of cement, it's timber, which constructs the set. You cannot pour it into a mold of any shape; its grain and springiness – as a builder knows – must be treated with respect. This has been fashioned into an allegory, but hasn't been sanded for splinters (which protrude from the shackle around Nicole Kidman's neck). Remember her labile features and how they have been poured into film after film after film.

Melancholia
Justine's face betrays almost no fruit. Michael's face is a changing map of emotions and attitudes. The evening, appalled, gets up and leaves, taking its scent with it: sweet, honeyed and metallic with green and spicy facets that result in the destruction of philosophy.

Dancer in the Dark
A cold little machine designed to sap feeling from eyes and hearts. Not ours, we have spent too long reading the little box that describes the art. Bjork is in hell. Lars stokes the fires then leaves. He scoots

away on the surface of this shallow film to its inevitable end, which
we could see from the start. Bjork didn't, her eye sight is fading
though her voice is bright as technicolour. Lars is no longer
listening, he won't even hear it.

Nymphomaniac

Buttery light fills the cinema. Later, old sweat, vague spices and
cum. Many wonder why pictures that are available for a woman's
body should be erotic. We know. Shia says he needs something that
came out of their own bodies. Tissue. Litter by the bin. Days later
they will find the bruises. Their shape sharpens as they become grey
and blue. They live inside the cut and travel. Leathery light around
three, you can see that she loves this picture. If you don't like that
it was beaten don't worry, he just found the poem on the floor tied
up in some fabric. It's also a little black and blue mark — not that he
wrote it to stand out, not that he filmed her like that. He lives outside
the cut, and travels. He has done what he likes to do, he writes from
abroad. The light is constantly changing. He wants little wounds that
will take a permanent record.

■

The Big G

It's said the Word came first so all of Genesis (from the Welsh family bible)
is here. But really the letter came first so there are lots of those too
and before that came the line – a line traced between points
and those points were stars. So Kamensky says: 'A Letter –
this is a completely separate planet of the universe (words are concepts).'

Before Kamensky came Blake and before him came Smart
who said that 'A is the beginning and the door to heaven.'
He's here as well and that door is the shape of a pyramid in the sky
like the one I saw that time in London.

Before Smart came Swedenborg – he was before Blake too
and Blake loved him like Genesis is loved with a Midrash;
a Midrash like Swedenborg wrote in *The Word of the Old Testament Explained*
fragments of this appear too – whispering '...spirits [who]
wrote by my hand and [for the sake of experience]
wrote words of which I had not thought.' Big thoughts
like Jung's Big Dreams

The Big G, 125cm x 105cm

like Schreber's Divine Rays,
like Zurn's Jasmine Man (none of them are here
but it would be good if they were.)

Letters radiate from a central 'g', 'For G is God,' says Smart,
says Kamensky, 'The Letter is an explosion, the Word –
a flock of explosions.' And the g's are the still point of many black wings
flapping all the other letters into existence
and 'Each Letter is a strictly individual world,
a symbolic concentration which gives us an exact definition
of internal and external essence.' Kamensky again – echoing Blake
echoing Swedenborg – his own echo chamber: '...when I was in interior sight,
those who were in exterior sight did not know what I saw;
it was a pyramid marvelously adorned.'
That pyramid again
flashing its warning at passing planes.

But that's going real deep into G – give me the waxy creased surface G
on the 'Big G Original Bubble Gum' wrapper – that's here too.
I've kept it for 22 years since Kenya, because that's what they called me there:
The Big G.

■

The morning after...

BLOOD	Fresh stain: Sponge with cold water. Old stain: Soak in water, then use permanganate and sulphite.
BONNEY'S BLUE	Hydrosulphite.
INKS	Contain lamp black and dye.
Duplicating Ink	Remove the former by smearing with oleic acid, steep in acetone, then smear with oleic acid and immerse in dilute ammonia. Wash with soap.
Rubber Stamp Ink	These have a water - soluble basis. Wash with water. Remove the dye with hydrosulphite.
PERSPIRATION	Wash with soap and water, followed by a bleaching agent if necessary.

TRINITROPHENOL   On skin or cotton: Wash with
warm water. On wool: redu-
cing agent.

[From *The Australian and New Zealand Pharmaceutical Formulary*, 1934]

■

Easter

They say
the scent of toast prods
the nose at our hour of death.
In heaven, I want to believe
every room smells like a
bakery—
I hope they serve more than just
hot cross buns, which is fine at Easter

but, forever?

Countdown

The audience in their numbers look deep
into the livestream, stunned, by its likeness
to the shallows of a blue sea, a sky within
reach, likeness itself. The audience, in their
numbers, count themselves, grouped by
a shared countdown, to ascend and transform,
from here (the mess created by a previous
audience) to there (a deep blue sky), promising
this audience to replace themselves of
themselves, in numbers, empty themselves
of content, and float in the empty place
of images, ascend and re-form deep
into the livestream, become likeness itself.

DAVID MUSGRAVE

■

The Project

Let's shut it down.
Let's shut down the project.
There are protocols to be disregarded,
but don't shred the paperwork.
Let's let it all happen, slowly
but not as slow as an ice age.

But if it isn't our project
can we shut it down? Sure
we can, just like folding
a newspaper up, tucking
the news away under an arm
or into the garbage. Maybe snow

is essentially nostalgic. Maybe
falling off a bicycle is natural.
Maybe ownership is a form of violence,
yeah, like violence is form
and violence has form. Definitely.
But I'd like to return to the project.

I think we should shut it down.
I think it has run its course.
There are only so many efficiency dividends
and property keeps on rising. Bubbles
nibble the meniscus of my beer
which is further evidence of what
needs to be done: within the message

vacuity is necessary, and vacuity
is a dark attractor. Let's keep going
and keep this in mind. A tennis ball
ages like a middle-aged man
but middle-aged men are not tennis balls

unless there is a 'let' every time
they think it's time to prove their relevance
like flies head-butting warm windows
or the dead sea of a white page filling with fly shit.
Ordinarily, that page would have been printed on
with schedules, memos, details of the project

but this no longer concerns us.
What matters is shutting down the project.
It no longer has a cost centre, but its costs
are incalculable. Shutting it down
is neither penny wise nor pound foolish:
it's entering the cave again, eyes wide open.

ANUPAMA PILBROW

Happiness Poem

Here I am eating a tasty
nectarine from my neighbour's tree
and I am eating round the dimple
of where it is eaten by birds ants
other insects and so on who also
like tasty things. Everything is in love
with sugar and I am licking all the juices
dripping down onto my pants and arms
and shoes I am licking them up and
licking my lips and soon enough I am
also eating inside the dimple eaten by
birds ants and so on and we
are sharing communion of fruit I
am tasting their mouths with my mouth
and I am eating the stone slowly and
grinding it into a paste in my teeth it
is an aphrodisiac.

Insect Poem

My auntie says look at
the difference in the colours of our skins
one lighter than the other (both brown)
in the hot air one sweaty the other dry
I hold her hand. We talk about race
I guess and I feel uncomfortable so does my
sister the fan hums my grandmother grandfather
have not died and they sit near and chat I
hold my auntie's hand cool and smooth. I hold
my sister's hand raised and hot damp her
hair sticks many insects have bitten her and
me but less me each bite like a growing
bulb pink and sore near to erupt. We scratch
until they scab yellow red shields I need to
pull away to get the itching treasure
underneath we cut our nails short and can't
get the treasure treasure upon treasure
erupting over our entire beings I want the
treasure. I do not want the treasure
temporary and diseased like eating so many
potato chips you regret
because of your stomach and head upset
from salt. My auntie's hand soothes me she asks
a riddle what colour do all human bodies share
in common white teeth I say whites of the eyes
oh pupils black pupils my sister says white
nails my auntie looks alarmed. No blood we
stroke and slap our bites for relief and wake
up bleeding small bubbles of blood on the
sheets not from the insects only from

ANUPAMA PILBROW

unconscious scratching I want to bite off
all the treasure mines and scratch them
forever and wish my skin calm smooth
like my auntie.

[Both poems published in *Body Poems*,Vagabond Press 2018]

Princes and other anxiolitics

Imaginary boyfriends become ever present, as the determinately ineffable. They live in 1) cyberhives, 2) anime speech bubbles, 3) imagined scenarios, 4) gated communities sometimes underground and known only by word of mouth, 5) in off-white creases of those we lock eyes with, 6) acquaintances, 7) new friends, 8) certain quicknesses, 9) skin collages, 10) closebys, who, so far, mask morality up to the point of convenience - 11) and the kind of faded, high glamour beauty shots on dressers that lose their pigmentation, living on beyond. It's the more at ease best friend of your older brother, a judicial kind of stranger, meeting totally tangentially in your dining room, while you sit adjacent. His stare is valuable but weirdly unmentioned. His haircut, more importantly, is totally horny. Your feet brush up against each other's two seconds more than was ever necessary - (a fantasy that's long been pornographied - the gays knew the market) imaginary boyfriends are nothing more than personal emotional investments. You really do want this rarified d*ck. Sometimes it holds value to submit to delirium when the time comes. If you believe enough in the compensation of another body eventually meeting up against yours, you have the vision for when love can materialise. Impossible crushes allow for opportunity to bloom, hope springing into eternities. But this is three pills fretfully downed, two moodboards away, five loaded radio songs too many. Sooner or later we all betray ourselves. They carry none of that threatening pretense and exist abundantly in a chalice of opportunity - If you want a stencil for a real thing they have a largesse, a movie face that previously only occupied your amygdala, finally - a real life doll of nervous energy becoming solidified as if in plasticine, a clean image to become an issued ultimatum, a distance like Nicholas Sparks really wanted.

JONNO REVANCHE

Yawning / cologne

A bathroom helps me lose you - some of
my emotions all lopsided
like Brecht, little
sacrament, shed roommates, bliss, continuum

That place fixed in my
head, forever referring to sense

Where I am a home
in your eclipse - tho your
mountain path goes
on, linking those tones among me

Non-memory, something solid, sophisticate
let free from the past

~

This night is ripe for the taste of terror
to let loose an ex boyfriend in house,

To later pick up a passing
piece in the smell of passerbys

Recover something
like jouissance

A fragment of
us, overture, moving

When I break, I do
it gradually, in your depth of vision;
when I depart, I
remember how far I've travelled

/

Your
scent is all I've ever
remembered: like a million
years in practice

You're never far
Away though I prick your thumb
On a map. Rub
your likeness around blur, we're
made to be this ineligible. Uncanny,
isn't it, that we
proved coupledom
outcome, even
when the odds were weighed up.

Your sinew, there! -
wrapped in a silk dress,
with a feathered torso and bright
wide gaze, looking, then we swap wardrobes.
What gets worn reveals
the notes we otherwise
wouldn't notice

Love,
in the time of
Viktor and Rolf

JUAN RUBÉN REYES

■

from Narrow Interior of the Shore

ROOM X

Immanent arch and
transfer

PAINTING IV

Scaffolding   —
pulleys. Ropes taut
in verticals. Bricks.
A fine, fine day. An
island. Ships. A line
of birds in flight.
Tiers and a red jug.
Layers   of

A dog beside you, drying off.
The promised holiday –
further up the hill,
visitors looking at photographs.

At the top of the pillars
a second sky and hill and you,
holding FLOWERS,
dropping things
that fall near the VISITORS.
And it has been a long time.

You write, "Sometimes
arches," inserting a lake
and Persian buttercups
in the foreground.

ANIMAL III

He paddles out
looking back at you,
to fetch the ball.

And you took a photograph
because he reminded
you of a SOFT THING.

A sealed
butterfly

ROOM X

A wave and another. The
rain on the vegetation
recording the
bipedal hunt

Confusion is a garden.

JUAN RUBÉN REYES

ANIMAL XII

The horses encircle the dog.
Observing. They do
not kindle anything.
Mostly, you gather from sight,
and from their SIGHT.

ROOM X

ANIMAL XXI

The dog looks through
the horses, who gather
in his outline.
Browns

and the textures of
bracken and fur.

Two hills frame
the dog TURNING.

As it turns the horses
run, leaving their bodies nearby.
We are incomplete and visible.

At the edge is where perception
falls away.

ROOM X

The visitors hold
the verticals and
there, before
and after,
is a splash.

He paddles out to fetch the ball.

Water
assembled

PAINTING XII

A circular hole in
the ice. A bird with
a red chest. Plains.
Thin   branches
through the sky.
Games. A wooden
door lain down at
an   angle

EMILY STEWART

■

Supply

extended interview   *worldview*

extended interview

extended interview

extended interview

extended interview

extended interview

extended interview

extended interview

extended interview

volume

volume

volume

volume

volume   *comfort————intelligence*

volume

volume

I read my vows in JavaSpeak
I read my vows in JavaSpeak
I read my vows in JavaSpeak
I read my vows in JavaSpeak
I read my vows in JavaSpeak
I read my vows in JavaSpeak
I read my vows in JavaSpeak
I read my vows in JavaSpeak
I read my vows in JavaSpeak
I read my vows in JavaSpeak
I read my vows in JavaSpeak
I read my vows in JavaSpeak
I read my vows in JavaSpeak

assent

scheme

$

device *device*

device *device*

device *device*

device *device*

device *device*

device *device*

task? *device* *device*

device *device*

EMILY STEWART

■

comfort———care

supertaster

<u>*scheme*</u>

climb back out

Constellation Points

I remember:

- Julian, an insistent cowboy, green-eyed; he made me a white Indian.

- his Cape Town English taught me vowels can meet at two oceans, circulate.

- rock-scrambling, a camp for Julian's church group. Atheists always abseil, but I let His hand guide me in the dark.

- his mothers' potpourri, a bungalow; she was a study in tolerance that afternoon: a painted gun clicked in my direction, and not for the first time.

- his departure for Perth; Jules, I said-- with a preternatural sense of how to author a memory--the West is no longer just the mind's saloon.

- last week thinking: Who watched us play colonies and push frontiers? The described past is an unwelcome metaphor, here, in real life's antipodes.

- not remembering Julian; my ceiling constellation glowed in the dark and I slept for the first time in a week, knowing that we shared certain stars.

- landing at Cape Town airport, inbound from Tambo, and driving straight to a restaurant on the foothills over Hout Bay, a Pet Nat sunset, platitudes exchanged with the boyfriend. Sydney is Cape Town, and isn't; I didn't remember Julian at all.

- reading Joe Brainard, two weeks later, at a cafe in Camp's Bay; as a vegan, champagne is the only way I can taste butter but here it is folded into scallops with garlic, just as his mother did while he watched from the kitchen table, just as all love is

DANIEL SWAIN

■

· remembered looking; a seeing when we can't, so real stars
glow in the dark; later, I'll see a man who is Julian, without
any resemblance, as we grind, I lose my phone and walk home
alone, unable to capture the fading stars or any other concept
of God.

The Aesthetes

Every time after sex when I insisted on your beauty, you thought I
was being disingenuous. Your reaction (irked, aroused, unmoved)
depended on who came first (me, you, N/A). We lack a thick
vocabulary of male beauty, I ventured, as the bin lipped a condom in
a tissue, nested.

*

*He had the kind of lonely adolescence that makes vanity
impossible,* I tell Nunzio, my therapist. *I convinced him of his
beauty.* The air-conditioning in his suite is broken, and it is summer
now (you left me, cruelly, at the beginning of Sydney's spring; I
remember emerging from my house to find straight boys wearing
shorts with a slightly kinky pride, their soles juicing jacaranda
leaves. Just handsomeness weighed against beauty). He bills by
the hour but Nunzio still takes the longest sip of water in clinical
history.

*

A week before you left me, showering together, we saw you: blue
white skin, collarbone well, a tapered mile between hip and dick.
Our eyes met in the bath mirror, a recursive looking, you turned the
tap: skinned water is floored wine and we drank Pinot Blanc on my
balcony, after drying Christopher Isherwood fell into bed with us,
he hit you in the face exactly unlike shower water. Kinky Chris does
poly bd. And Herbert Tobias watched, from the poster above my bed,
Take him down, you suggested, and I refused. I'll tell my therapist
semi-truthfully, you never understood my aesthetics. That evening
we ate blueberries with South African Chenin, sex again, this time,
the last time, with a single finger; you had tears in your eyes when
you came, and an awareness arrived: you can argue over beauty but
beauty is always an argument.

■

Sonnet: Thanksgiving

(after Sherman Alexie)

1. The snow came early. 2. I'm talking before Thanksgiving early.
3. My grandmother, who hated snow, was good at giving thanks.
4. She was better at making trouble. 5. Take Thanksgiving 1982
when we argued the merits of right-to-life vs right-to-choose, and
she said to Aunt Francie, "But you had an abortion." 6. That must
have been like 1941, before Uncle Pete signed up and went off to
the war. 7. What if Pete died, they must have been thinking. 8. I'm
imagining that, but what if he had and Aunt Francie had the baby
but no husband in Williamsburg, Brooklyn, 1942, during the war?
9. Now we have wars all the time, many more wars. 10. And more
abortions, more Thanksgivings, more snow on the ground. 11. And
more fire. 12. More floods. 13. Even lava. 14. Today, on a platform
waiting for the uptown R, I get a call from a debt collector. It was a
wrong number, but she was so convincing I said, "All right, I'll pay."
Then the train came.

Sonnet: If I Pushed It In

I love to watch you shave your legs without
a care for nicks and cuts, the shave cream thick
and white and the razor sliding blithely
along the shin and up the elegant
calf, love to watch you tap the cream and hair
into the tub filled with warm water, clouds
floating on the surface and the leg hair
stubbles forming phrases that disappear
like smoke rings on windy days. How you make
magic that way, other ways, too, each time
you shave your legs without a care for nicks
and cuts or the things they talk about on
that radio plugged in at the tub's edge.
What would happen if I pushed it in?

TIM TOMLINSON

Aubade: Barracks and Burgundy

Another dawn in the French Quarter and
the greasy flow of the night turns stiff.
A kitten with eye-pus cowers inside

a go-cup, and roaches the size of
Churchill cigars don't even bother to hide.
No one making groceries in the Li'l General

can remember what the fuck they went in
for, and at 710 Royal a guy
in a coma wears a t-shirt that says

"This Face Seats Five—Comfortably." Something half
digested crusts on his soul patch and his
liver squeaks out from his ribs like a bubble

in the seam of an old football. Inside
the Abbey the women have black eyes and
cigarette packs rolled up in the sleeves

of Lynyrd Skynyrd t-shirts, and the bats
are so stuffed with termites they practically
crawl home below lampposts that don't wear

halos anymore. A rattle of Mardi Gras
beads from a balcony on Barracks Street
a ceiling fan spins in a room where

the tone-arm of an ancient Garrard digs
grooves into a Fats Domino record.
Beneath a banana tree near Bienville

an on-duty cop plops his cock into
the face hidden inside the window of a
Dodge Dart, while a Jackson Square tour guide

empties the pockets of tourists passed-out
in the buggy of his mule-drawn carriage.
And over at the Rebel Arms on Decatur

a teenager from New York sleeps with his
face pressed against a jukebox playing "Ruby"
by Ray Charles over and over and not

even the bartender thinks she's had enough.

ED WRIGHT

Tunnel Leaks

Driving through the Sydney Harbour Tunnel
My wife is talking in mother tongue on the phone
Above are fish and mud
a few accountants from the eighties
perhaps even a cruise ship
where a rich American geriatric is processing
a second martini with his second liver.
His wife beside him is photographing the view
from the balcony of their state room –
the Opera House is like a sailing ship or slices of
a white orange he reads,
apparently they forgot
to leave enough room for the orchestra –
all that effort and no place for the second fiddles –
people – if you want it done properly then you have
to do it yourself. Decades of assertion have been
hollowed by retirement to ritual – his wife says yes –
it seems everyone has forgotten
his importance, last night
he sent his steak back to the kitchen –
more than anything to feel the cause and effect of his voice.
I like the bridge better, useful, he says,
she nods – this afternoon she has plans
to go ashore and buy her grandson
a boomerang.

Out from under the harbour
and lacking time we continue to the airport,
beneath the towers of the financiers
the traffic stalls, will we make it?
Less than ten hours now to Singapore
where they will bury the President
(a miracle worker of the mud and sea,
who once sat three chairs away from the
rich cruiser at a function and refused
to hear his pitch) while we are in transit
between this place where the politicians
are almost irrelevant, and that place
where it is hard to speak
the President s name.

ED WRIGHT

The Mower

I died stubbornly
it was the most exciting thing
that had happened to me for years
mowing the lawn in a thunderstorm
when the lightning struck I was amazed
Eliza was wanting to go to the mall
I was using the grass as an excuse
hard to argue with a mower

when she saw me clutch my chest and drop
I heard her scream though – it was a relief
I remembered our long love and felt special
as the traffic parted for the ambulance
it would have been nice if the sirens were
made of Thelonious Monk, but they
were fast enough to bring me back
and I've never enjoyed waking up
and being called a bloody idiot more.

[Published as 'Cut Grass' in *Brew*, Poetry at the Pub 2018]

Float tank

Rosie reckons it's like the '90s again
and there is a loop to it
how ritual recycles time to create
illusions of timelessness.
The whales sing you in
to spirals of self
a going round gossamer
it's dark in here
fear is never far away
that's the price of entry
not just to this cocoon, don't panic;
it's only from the inside that we can escape
the done deal of ourselves
only by going to the duller repetitions,
thuds of the heart, the in outs of the breath …

the whale song is returning now
I could have gone further but it's time
to open the hatch of the egg.

This anthology is a collection of new and previously published works by writers who appeared at Cuplet Poetry Night (Newcastle NSW) in 2018. Cuplet began in August 2018 as an experiment, and has grown and flourished in the local literary community. I hope you have enjoyed these collated works which show the breadth and diversity of the fine poetry we've been lucky to enjoy in this first thrilling year. Onwards, to 2019!

I would like to extend thanks to David Musgrave and all the directors at Puncher & Wattmann who agreed to publish this anthology out of the blue with the greatest equanimity, and trusted me with its editing, type-setting and design.

Special thanks go to all the talented and hard-working poets who got these works to me in record time. You have made it the remarkable collection of contemporary and ground-breaking poetry that it is.

Thank you also to Toby Fitch, who shared his expertise and support from the start of the Cuplet project.

To all those who have come to Cuplet events - and especially those who have donated to the Cuplet Clams - thank you! This is a direct result of your support, and I couldn't have done it without you. Newcastle really is a hotspot of poetry. And to The Beaumont, who have housed us from the beginning, I am eternally grateful.

Lastly, thank you to the University of Newcastle's Centre for 21st Century Humanities. This fantastic centre provided start-up funds supporting, among other things, the production and printing of this book, which is a testament to their generosity.

— Claire Albrecht, December 2018

Editor's Note

CHRIS BROWN is a poet and teacher. His poems have appeared in *Southerly, Overland, The Age, Cordite* and *Otoliths*, among other publications. He is a PhD student at Newcastle University and editor of Puncher & Wattmann's *Slow Loris* Chapbook Series.

MICHELLE CAHILL lives in Sydney and is the author of *The Herring Lass* and *Letter to Pessoa* which was awarded the UTS Glenda Adams Award. She was a CAL/UOW Poetry Fellow at Kingston Writing School. Her acclaimed collection *Vishvarupa* will be republished by UWAP in 2019.

A.J. CARRUTHERS is an experimental poet, performer and literary critic, author of *Stave Sightings: Notational Experiments in North American Long Poems* (Cham: Palgrave Macmillan, 2017). The first volume of a lifelong long poem *AXIS Book 1: Areal*, appeared from Vagabond in 2014, and excerpts from it appeared as *The Blazar Axes* (Calgary: Spacecraft Press, 2018). In 2017 he was appointed Lecturer at the Australian Studies Centre in SUIBE, Shanghai.

AMELIA DALE's most recent book *Constitution* (Inken Publisch) won Mascara Literary Review's Avant Garde award for poetry. She is editor in chief of Stale Objects dePress, on the editorial boards of *Rabbit Poetry Journal* and *Cordite Poetry Review* and a lecturer in the Australian Studies Centre in SUIBE.

TRICIA DEARBORN has been widely published in literary journals in Australia, overseas and online. She is on the editorial board of *Plumwood Mountain*, a journal of ecopoetry. Her third collection, *Autobiochemistry*, is forthcoming from UWA Publishing in 2019.

BENJAMIN DODDS is the author of *Regulator* (Puncher & Wattmann Poetry, 2014). His work has appeared in *Best Australian Poetry*, *Meanjin*, *Southerly*, *Cordite* and on Radio National's *Poetica* program.

TOBY FITCH is poetry editor of *Overland*. He was awarded his PhD at the University of Sydney in 2016. His books include *Rawshock*, which won the Grace Leven Prize for Poetry 2012, *The Bloomin' Notions of Other & Beau* and, most recently, *ILL LIT POP*.

KERI GLASTONBURY is a Senior Lecturer in Creative Writing at The University of Newcastle. She is a widely published Australian poet and has received numerous grants from the Australia Council. Her most recent collection is *Newcastle Sonnets* (Giramondo, 2018), an antipodean, regional queering of Ted Berrigan's New York-based *The Sonnets*.

JANETTE HOPPE's poetry is a reflection of her Australian and New Zealand Maori heritage. Her work has been published in Australia, New Zealand and the United Kingdom. In 2011 Janette launched Papatuanuku Press, an underground publishing project that creates poetry events and books that raise funds to support charities such as Beyond Blue and The White Ribbon Foundation.

HOLLY ISEMONGER was the joint winner of the 2016 Overland Judith Wright Poetry Prize. She is the author of the chapbook *Hip Shifts* (If A Leaf Falls Press) and *Deluxe Paperweight* (Stale Objects dePress). She co-edited the 'DIFFICULT' issue of *Cordite* and has performed at Sydney Writers Festival and Brisbane Writers Festival. She can be found at hisemonger.tumblr.com and tweets as @hisemonger.

DR GARETH JENKINS is currently editing Anthony Mannix's first collection of writing, due for publication with Puncher & Wattmann in 2018. His own first full-length collection of poetry, *Recipes for the Disaster,* will be published by Five Islands Press in 2019. He makes text-based art at Square One Studios in Sydney.

ŠIME KNEŽEVIĆ a writer and artist. His poems have appeared in *Ambit, Australian Poetry Journal, Cordite Poetry Review, Magma, SAND, The Stockholm Review of Literature,* and elsewhere. *The Hostage* won the 2018 Subbed In Chapbook Prize and will be published in 2019. He lives in Sydney.

DAVID MUSGRAVE is a poet, novelist, publisher and critic who lives in "Wazzatah" with his family and lectures at the University of Newcastle. He is the founding publisher of Puncher & Wattmann press, has authored and edited over ten books, and has twice won the Newcastle Poetry Prize.

ANUPAMA PILBROW is co-editor of Narrm/Melbourne-based digital journal *The Suburban Review.* Her debut chapbook *Body Poems* was released as part of Vagabond Press' deciBels 3 series. Anupama's poetry, essays, and reviews can be found in local and international journals. Her work deals with dialogue, exchange, family, and gross stuff.

JONNO REVANCHE is a writer and multi-hyphenate artist person currently living on gadigal land in Sydney. They're interested in such light-hearted and enjoyable literary themes as isolation, despair, climate catastrophe, depersonalisation, and the collapse of contemporary life as we understand it.

JUAN RUBÉN REYES is a poet and artist with an interest in experimental fiction and poetry. He is currently undertaking doctoral studies at the University of Newcastle examinng facticity and the translation of observed events into language in Charles Reznikoff's *Testimony: The United States (1885-1915): Recitative.*

EMILY STEWART is poetry editor at Giramondo Publishing and a doctoral candidate at Western Sydney University. She is the author of *Knocks* (Vagabond Press 2016) and several chapbooks including *The Internet Blue* (Firstdraft) and *Australia's Largest DIY* (SOd Press).

DANIEL SWAIN is a queer writer based in Sydney. His poetry has been published in *Rabbit* and *Cordite*, his prose has been published by *Archer. Junkee* and the *Sydney Morning Herald.* He presented on Frank O'Hara and Wayne Koestenbaum at the Queer Legacies, New Solidarities conference in Melbourne in 2018.

TIM TOMLINSON is co-founder of New York Writers Workshop and co-author of its popular text, *The Portable MFA in Creative Writing.* He is also the author of *Yolanda: An Oral History in Verse, Requiem for the Tree Fort I Set on Fire* (poetry), and *This Is Not Happening to You* (short fiction). He teaches in the Global Liberal Studies Program at NYU.

ED WRIGHT has published a chapbook of poetry, *The Empty Room,* with Vagabond Press and a full volume of poetry, *When Sky Becomes the Space Inside Your Head,* while individual poems and stories have been published in journals such as *Meanjin, Island, Overland, Cordite* and *Snorkel* He lives in Newcastle where he is, among other things, the Director of the The Creative Word Shop.

The Editor ▮▮▮▮▮▮▮▮▮▮▮▮▮▮▮▮▮▮▮▮

CLAIRE ALBRECHT is writing her PhD at the University of Newcastle. Her current work investigates the connections between poetry/ photography and sex/politics. Claire's poems appear in Australian print and online journals including *Cordite Poetry Review, Overland Literary Journal, Plumwood Mountain, The Suburban Review* and others. Her manuscript *sediment* was shortlisted for the 2018 Subbed In chapbook prize, and the poem 'mindfulness' won the Secret Spaces prize. Her debut chapbook *pinky swear* launched in October 2018.

www.ingramcontent.com/pod-product-compliance
Lightning Source LLC
Chambersburg PA
CBHW030855090426
42737CB00009B/1238